OCEANS ALIVE

Sea Stars

by Ann Herriges

BELLWETHER MEDIA • MINNEAPOLIS, MN

Note to Librarians, Teachers, and Parents:

Blastoff! Readers are carefully developed by literacy experts and combine standards-based content with developmentally appropriate text.

Level 1 provides the most support through repetition of high-frequency words, light text, predictable sentence patterns, and strong visual support.

Level 2 offers early readers a bit more challenge through varied simple sentences, increased text load, and less repetition of high-frequency words.

Level 3 advances early-fluent readers toward fluency through increased text and concept load, less reliance on visuals, longer sentences, and more literary language.

Whichever book is right for your reader, Blastoff! Readers are the perfect books to build confidence and encourage a love of reading that will last a lifetime!

This edition first published in 2007 by Bellwether Media.

No part of this publication may be reproduced in whole or in part without written permission of the publisher. For information regarding permission, write to Bellwether Media Inc., Attention: Permissions Department, Post Office Box 1C, Minnetonka, MN 55345-9998.

Library of Congress Cataloging-in-Publication Data
Herriges, Ann.
   Sea stars / by Ann Herriges.
     p. cm. — (Blastoff! readers) (Oceans alive!)
Summary: "Simple text and supportive images introduce beginning readers to sea stars. Intended for students in kindergarten through third grade."
   Includes bibliographical references and index.
   ISBN-10: 1-60014-021-1 (hardcover : alk. paper)
   ISBN-13: 978-1-60014-021-1 (hardcover : alk. paper)
   1. Starfishes—Juvenile literature. I. Title. II. Series.

QL384.A8H465 2008
593.9'3—dc22   2006001993

Text copyright © 2007 by Bellwether Media.
Printed in the United States of America.

Table of Contents

Sea stars live in oceans all over the world.

Sea stars come in many sizes
and colors.

Sea stars have a hard,
bumpy body.

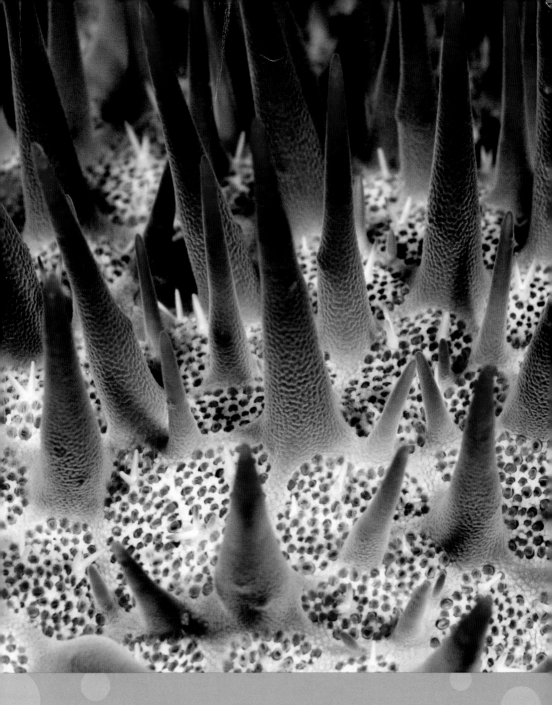

Sharp **spines** cover their body.

Sea stars have a mouth in the middle of their body.

Sea stars have arms
called **rays**.

Sea stars have at least
five rays.

Some sea stars have many
more rays.

Sea stars can lose their rays.

Then new rays grow.

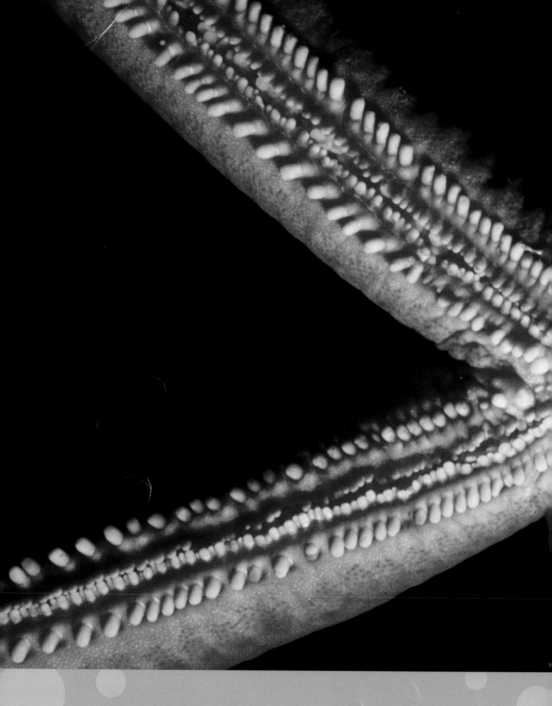

Sea stars have a **groove** on each ray.

Each groove has rows
of feet.

Sea stars use their feet to crawl and to hold onto rocks.

Sea stars use their feet to help them eat animals that have **shells**.

A sea star pulls on each side of the shell with its feet. The shell opens.

The sea star pushes its
stomach through its mouth
and into the shell.

The sea star's stomach feeds on the soft food inside the shell.

The sea star pulls in its stomach. It leaves the empty shell behind.

Glossary

groove—a long line in the surface of something; the grooves on a sea star reach from its mouth to the tip of each ray.

ray—an arm that grows out from the center of a sea star; rays can be short and wide or long and narrow.

shell—a hard outer covering; many animals that sea stars eat have shells; they include clams, oysters, and mussels.

spines—hard, sharp growths that stick out from the body of an animal for protection

To Learn More

AT THE LIBRARY

Andreae, Giles. *Commotion in the Ocean*. Wilton, Conn.: Tiger Tales, 2002.

Douglas, Lloyd G. *Starfish*. Danbury, Conn.: Children's Press, 2005.

Hurd, Edith Thacher. *Starfish*. New York: Harper Trophy, 2000.

Logue, Mary. *Sea Stars*. Chanhassen, Minn.: Child's World, 2005.

Louchard, Antonin. *Little Star*. New York: Hyperion, 2003.

Ridinger, Gayle. *A Star at the Bottom of the Sea*. Milwaukee, Wis.: Gareth Stevens, 2002.

ON THE WEB

Learning more about sea stars is as easy as 1, 2, 3.

1. Go to www.factsurfer.com

2. Enter "sea stars" into search box.

3. Click the "Surf" button and you will see a list of related web sites.

With factsurfer.com, finding more information is just a click away.

Index

The photographs in this book are reproduced through the courtesy of: davies & starr/Getty Images, front cover; Stephen Frink/Getty Images, p. 4; Darrell Gulin/Getty Images, p. 5; Beth Dixson/Getty Images, p. 6; C. Wolcott Henry III/Getty Images, p. 7; Margo Steley/Alamy, p. 8; Premium Stock/Getty Images, p. 9; Eric Bean/Getty Images, p. 10; David Wrobel/Getty Images, p. 11; Stephen Frink Alamy, pp. 12-13; Jeff Rotman/Getty Images, pp. 14-15; David Doubilet/Getty Images, pp. 16-17; David Fleetham/Alamy, p. 18; Andre Seale/Alamy, p. 19; Chris Howes/Wild Places Photography/Alamy, pp. 20-21.